Manuela Dunn Mascetti

KALI

GODDESS OF CREATION AND DESTRUCTION

CHRONICLE BOOKS
SAN FRANCISCO

TEXT BY Manuela Dunn Mascetti

DESIGN BY Bullet Liongson

Manufactured in China

Typeset in Minion

ISBN 0-8118-3426-3

10 9 8 7 6 5 4 3 2 1

Distributed in Canada by

RAINCOAST BOOKS

9050 Shaughnessy Street

Vancouver, BC V6P 6E5

CHRONICLE BOOKS LLC

85 Second Street

San Francisco, CA 94105

www.chroniclebooks.com

Table of Contents

Introduction

*Kali manifested herself for the annihilation of demonic male
power in order to restore peace and equilibrium. For a long
time* asuric *(demonic) forces had been dominating and
oppressing the world. Even the powerful gods were helpless
and suffered defeat at their hands. They fled pell-mell in
utter humiliation, a state hardly fit for the divine. Finally
they prayed in desperation to the Daughter of the Himalayas
to save gods and men alike. The gods sent forth their energies
as a stream of fire, and from these energies emerged the
Great Goddess Durga. In the great battle to destroy the most
arrogant and truculent man-beasts, the Goddess Kali sprang
forth from the brow of Durga to join in the fierce fighting.*
—AJIT MOOKERJEE, Kali: The Feminine Force.

In modern India, Kali has many followers; she presides over
temples throughout the country, and a literary genre of
devotional poetry is dedicated solely to her. She is one of
the primary goddesses worshiped in India today, especially
by women and noted mystics such as Ramakrishna, perhaps
the most famous Indian saint of this century.

Kali's myths and stories are as rich and varied as Hindu
mythology itself. As we shall see, she is related to—and
sometimes one with—other great female divinities of

Kali

Hinduism: Durga, Devi, Shakti, Parvati, Kalika. She represents the vision of sacred woman, the divine force, the vital breath. Kali is the epitome of femaleness, and in worshiping her, women devotees lose the patriarchal standards of beauty and behavior and enjoy primordial female energy in its purest form. Once one realizes unity with Kali, the goddess no longer appears terrible and frightening.

According to Hindu tradition, we are now living in the Kali Yuga, the fourth and last of the great ages. Each Yuga lasts 432,000 divine years (each divine year equal to 360 of our own years), and the Kali Yuga began in 3102 BCE. Righteousness pervaded the universe when it was first created by the gods, but in the Kali Yuga that primordial goodness has dwindled to one quarter of its original level, spiritual efforts are poor, knowledge has been forgotten, and evil dominates. Disease, fatigue, anger, hunger, fear, and despair gain ground; humanity has no goal. This time of darkness is the moment for the resurgence of the divine feminine spirit that brings light back to the world. That restoration is the principal task of Kali, the great dangerous goddess. In Hindu mythology, it is said that she sprang from the brow of the goddess Durga during a battle to annihilate demonic masculine power. Hindus believe the same eternal battle is occurring now, in our own time of darkness, and that a new emergence of the Feminine will return the Earth to balance.

Kali represents an overwhelming intensity and a mighty strength. When she sprang forth from Durga's brow, the skies were filled with a mighty roar. She is both good and evil—undivided—as were most prehistoric goddesses before patriarchy robbed them of their sexual and destructive powers. Kali is an ambivalent goddess who destroys in order to create a better world for us, and as such her actions are like those of a fierce mother.

Although Kali is often portrayed in her warrior aspect as cruel and horrific, with a lolling red tongue and necklace of severed heads, she is not solely a destructive force. Kali is also a creator and nurturing goddess whose battles are for a just cause: to free us from unconscious forces that cause suffering. She is in this sense the personification of mother love and feminine energy, known in the Hindu religion as *shakti*.

Kali is an intoxicating embodiment of primal energy. Her myth dates back to the beginning of Hindu recorded history, first chronicled in the great Indian epic the *Mahabharata*

and in mythological stories known as the *Puranas*. The
most famous story of Kali's accomplishments is found in
the sixth-century text *Markandeya Purana*.

By the eleventh century Kali had gained another dimen-
sion as one of the principal goddesses of Tantric philosophy,
thus becoming a real spiritual force for her devotees rather
than merely a goddess whose deeds were recorded in
Hindu myths. Kali's form and her quality of nonduality are
praised and used as meditation tools in Tantra. Kali is also
the primary force in kundalini yoga, a Tantric method of
raising energy through the seven chakras to meet the divine,
practiced today in the United States and Europe, as well as
in Hinduism's native regions.

During one of her mythic battles, Kali was cut up in
pieces that were scattered throughout the subcontinent,
where her devotees found them and built temples in her
honor, through their devotion linking each piece and
temple to the rest in a great chain that reconnects her body
and energy. One of the most famous Kali temples is in
Calcutta, on the banks of the river Ganges, where every
day men and women worship the great goddess of creation
and destruction:

The temple serves as a slaughterhouse, for those performing
the sacrifice retain their animals, leaving only the head in the
temple as a symbolic gift, while the blood flows to the Goddess.
For to the Goddess is due the lifeblood of all creatures—since
it is she who has bestowed it—and that is why the beast must
be slaughtered in her temple. In the mud compounded of
blood and earth, the heads of the animals are heaped up like
trophies before the statue of the Goddess, while those
sacrificing return home for a family banquet of the bodies of
their animals. The head signifies the whole, the total sacrifice.
—**ERICH NEUMAN**, The Great Mother

Kali's power and popularity are derived from her link
to the great Mother Goddess of prehistoric worship and
from her transformation into a "modern" goddess of
dramatic dimensions who is still venerated today. It is said
that when the soul worships a divinity it becomes like a
child, and the divinity like an embracing mother. This is
eminently true of Kali, who embraces us all as the great
mother.

Your personal experience of this powerful female
divinity may begin with the statuette you find in this box,
a traditional Hindu representation of Kali. You can place
her on your home altar, by your bedside, or on your desk

or bookshelf, as long as she stands alone and is not close to any representation of a different god or goddess who might detract from her mighty power.

Kali will help you destroy old patterns, shatter entrenched situations that cause unhappiness, and transform relationships into renewed and deepened bonds. She chases away your demons and the negative emotions that keep you from evolving and choosing happiness in your life's circumstances.

Let Kali remind you that you can transform your life: You have full power over the negative and can turn ugliness into beauty, bad into good, darkness into light.

Let Kali bless your life with her astounding primordial force and help you make existence the dream it was always meant to be.

The Force of the Feminine

Beginning in the Paleolithic era of Old Europe, from circa 7000 to 3500 BCE, humankind worshiped an all-powerful Mother Goddess, believed to be the originator of people, animals, plants, sky, earth, life, death, and rebirth. Amongst our hunting and gathering ancestors, seventy-five to eighty percent of the group's subsistence was derived from women's gathering activities. The oldest tools ever found in ancient sites are women's digging sticks. Women were probably the first users and domesticators of fire. They were also the first potters, weavers, textile dyers, and hide tanners, the first to gather medicinal plants, and the first to record time, measured according to their menses and the phases of the moon. Kali incarnates many qualities of the all-powerful prehistoric Mother Goddess dating back to a matriarchal era that lasted for millennia before the advent of patriarchy and its male-biased religion.

Everything in existence reflected the presence of the great Mother Goddess. Our very early ancestors, whose detailed religious practice is now lost in the mists of time, have left us primal images and symbols of her, which we

trace back through archaeology. From the Upper Paleolithic to the Middle Paleolithic period, the only god image painted on rock, carved in stone, or sculpted in clay was the image of a human female. The depictions that remain are those of a world imagined as female: the cave as womb; the mother as a pregnant earth; the magical fertile female as the mother of all animals; a prehistoric Venus, like the Venus of Laussel from a cave complex in France, standing with the horn of the moon upraised in her hand. In the first attempts at agriculture, prehistoric humans could follow the life of a seed from the moment it was first planted under the earth—seen as the womb of the Goddess—to its germination and growth, to its maturity as nourishing food, and to its return to the Earth to begin the cycle anew. Human life was understood to follow the same cycle, and prehistoric tombs show that the dead were buried covered in ochre, representing the red blood of the Mother Goddess, and in the fetal position, awaiting a new life. In the sky, the moon too followed a cycle, from the half crescent that symbolized young life, to fullness, to the waning moon that denoted old age.

The Mother Goddess religion dominated prehistory. In archaeological remains of the period, the Goddess is ubiquitous: In pottery and sacred statuettes, in dwellings, caves, and sacred hearths, in all that we can glean of lifestyles and veneration modes, everything attests to the religion of the Great Goddess, which was a primordial attempt on humanity's part to understand and live in harmony with the beauty and wonder of Nature.

Yet millennia of Goddess worship were buried with the coming of patriarchy. The cattle-herding Indo-European tribes that, wave upon wave, overran the territories of Old Europe from the fourth millennium BCE brought with them male-dominated pantheons that contrasted sharply with the Goddess deities of the Paleolithic era. Indo-European religious beliefs were embodied by horse-riding warrior gods of the thundering and shining skies or of the swampy under-world, and their goddesses were not creators but beauties, "Venuses," brides of the sky gods. The Indo-European mode of life was based on patriarchy; domination of Nature through small-scale agriculture and animal husbandry; the domestication of the horse; and skill with weapons such as the bow and arrow, spear, and dagger. This became the dominant culture from roughly 4300 to 1500 BCE; male gods and a patriarchal society that had little care for living in

harmony with Nature replaced the old religion of the Mother-Goddess-Creator. Nevertheless, the old Goddess religion and its symbols survived as undercurrents in various areas, and many of these symbols are still present today, perhaps nowhere as evident as in India.

India is the only country where the Goddess is still widely worshiped in our times, its tradition dating back to the Harappan culture of circa 3000 BCE. This Indus Valley civilization, named after its first discovered city, Harappa, flourished in the western part of South Asia in what today is Pakistan and western India. The Indus Valley was home to the largest of the four ancient urban civilizations—Egypt, Mesopotamia, India, and China. It was not discovered until the 1920s, and most of its ruins, including major cities, have yet to be excavated. However, Mother Goddess and fertility cults seem to have constituted its major forms of worship, just as they did in Old Europe at the same time.

In many parts of India, stone megaliths, standing stones, and womblike caves carved with Goddess symbols survive from that prehistoric time and are still objects of worship. In Bolhai, in the Central Indian state of Madhya Pradesh, there is a Harappan megalith representing the great Mother

Goddess in the form of a red-coated oval stone that has been worshiped continuously for about five thousand years. In Sanskrit, the language of Hindu sacred scriptures, the word for a sanctuary is *garbha-grha*, or "womb-chamber." Today, every village in India has its Mother Goddess and cult objects, and the majority of village deities are female. For the villagers who worship Mother Goddesses such as Kali, religious life centers on rituals intended to restore fertility to the soil in this still predominantly agricultural society; the origin of their deities can be traced back thousands and thousands of years. Goddesses dwell in trees, by the water's edge, in stones, and in shrines, appearing in many different forms and under many different names. Sometimes a goddess shares her name with a whole region, and even the vast subcontinent is known as "Mother India." Thus a goddess in India is not just a mysterious force whose worship, a remnant of antiquity, is now on the wane— on the contrary, she is the very soil, the all-creating and all-consuming.

Shakti and Shiva

By you this universe is born, by you this universe is created.
By you it is protected, O Devi. By you it is consumed at the end.
You who are eternally the form of the whole world,
At the time of creation you are the form of creative force,
At the time of preservation you are the form of protective power,
And at the time of the dissolution of the world
You are the form of the destructive power.
You are the Supreme Knowledge, as well as ignorance,
Intellect, and contemplation.
—from "Devi Mahatmya" in the *Markandeya Purana*

In the Hindu religion, the powerful and all-dominating feminine sacred force is known as *shakti*. The Sanskrit word refers to the primal creative principle underlying the cosmos, the energizing momentum of the divine, of every being, of every thing. The whole universe is a manifestation of this force. *Shakti* is Nature's first impulse, which is to produce the feminine: This ancient concept seems to correspond to the modern Western understanding that everyone's life is originally female, and only when the male hormone is added to the fetus in the womb does gender change to male.

The male counterpart to the embodied female deity

Shakti is Shiva, one of the greatest of gods, who with Vishnu and Brahma forms a triumvirate, the *trimurti*, a single body with three godly shapes. Shiva is the god of destruction, lord of ashes and oil, and the ultimate ascetic and protector of yogis. The play between primordial female and male forces is represented in Hindu myth as the marriage between Shakti and Shiva, whose interaction destroys and creates the entire universe in an eternal cycle. The sound of the interplay between Shakti and Shiva is *aum*, the soundless sound that is heard to reverberate throughout the universe when one is in meditation. The vibrancy between them also generates the *gunas*, or three fundamental qualities of the universe: *sattva*, *rajas*, and *tamas*. In the physical world, *sattva* embodies what is pure and unalloyed, *rajas* embodies activity, and *tamas* embodies heaviness and immobility (like water, steam, and ice). If the three qualities are in perfect balance, nothing is manifested—neither creation nor destruction. Once their balance is disturbed, however, creation becomes manifest.

Shakti, as the life-giver of the forces of the universe, powers even Shiva. It is said that she is the "i" in Shiva's name. Without the "i," Shiva becomes *shva*, which in

Sanskrit means corpse. Without Shakti, even Shiva is powerless to create and to preside over the other gods.

The Myth of Kali

The Hindus received their religion through revelations known as the Vedas, given directly from divine powers to the great *rishis*, or ancient seers. The *rishis* who transmitted them either heard or saw these very pure thought forms, but were not the original authors of the ideas. Perhaps because the Vedas owe their origin and authority to no one, they are considered the most untainted, most distilled form of the sacred. The *rishis* put the Vedas into Sanskrit— a "pure" language used only to speak of the divine—when they recorded the revelations. The Vedas are considered the oldest books of humankind, dating in their written form back to 1500 BCE but transmitted orally from one generation of *rishis* to the next from much earlier; they are thought to be the source of many principles underlying other religions. The texts speak of eternal truths and are the embodiment of supreme divine knowledge.

For millennia, under the special tutelage of *rishis* and priests, the Vedas were popularized through the Puranas, also known as the "friendly treatises." Written from about the fourth century BCE to about 1000 CE, the Puranas are designed to impress upon ordinary people the teachings of the Vedas and to generate in them devotion to god through concrete examples, myths, stories, legends, allegories, and chronicles of great historical events, and lives of saints, kings, and great men. It was during the time the Puranas were written that belief in a dark female goddess was first established.

In the *Markandeya Purana*, believed to have been written in the sixth century CE, we find the first text chronicling the embodiment of *shakti* energy in its dark and frightening form of Kali. The "Devi Mahatmya" section of this Purana marks the literary debut of Kali's myths and stories.

Kali is said to have sprung forth from the brow of Durga, the "unfathomable one" and one of the oldest manifestations of *shakti* power, during one of the battles between the gods and the demons. Durga's name underscores her independent, fiercely matriarchal status, like that of the ancient goddesses of Old Europe and the Harappa Civilization before the advent of Indo-European patriarchal beliefs stripped goddesses of their stronger, harsher qualities. Kali is considered the darker form of Durga, and thus also intensely independent and mighty.

জয়কালী রথ প্রিন্টিং ওয়ার্কস

Kali

In the myths of the "Devi Mahatmya," Kali is represented as a woman with black skin and four arms; in one hand she has a sword and in another the head of a demon she has slain, while with the remaining two she gives encouragement to her worshipers. She is adorned with a necklace of skulls and for earrings wears two dead bodies; her only clothing is a girdle made of dead men's hands, and her tongue protrudes from her mouth. Her eyes are red, her face and breasts smeared with blood. She stands with one foot on her thigh and the other on the breast of her husband, most often represented by Shiva.

Kali's blackness symbolizes her all-embracing, all-consuming quality, because black is the color into which all others merge. As all colors disappear into black, so all names and forms disappear into her. The Indian mystic Ramakrishna Paramahansa (1836 to 1886 CE) described Kali's blackness thus:

> *Is Kali, my Divine Mother, of a black complexion?*
> *She appears black because she is viewed from a distance;*
> *But when intimately known she is no longer so.*
> *The sky appears blue at a distance, but look at it close by*
> *And you will find it has no color.*

The water of the ocean looks blue at a distance,
But when you go near and take it in your hand,
You find that it is colorless.
—The Gospel of Sri Ramakrishna

Durga, Kali, and the War Against the Demons

According to the "Devi Mahatmya," the *asuras*, the dark yet divine demons of Hindu mythology, had overrun the world, and the gods were angry. In waging war against the *asuras*, the gods lost battle after battle and were growing exhausted and impotent in their fight to regain control of the world. They decided to create a female deity who would conquer the demons; to this end they combined their energies and merged into a huge ball of fire shooting light in all directions, and in the tumult and chaos the goddess Durga was born.

The new deity projected immense power and might. She was three-eyed, all-seeing, and adorned with the crescent moon. Her many arms held weapons and shields, emblems of good fortune, jewels and ornaments, and strings of beads, and all these were offered to the gods as sacrifices to win their favor in the great battle she was about to undertake. Seated on her tiger in readiness for war with the demonic

forces, her body blazing with the light of a thousand suns, Durga is the most powerful incarnation of female energy in Hindu mythology.

The world trembled and the seas were whipped to a great foaming frenzy as Durga engaged the demon chief, Mahisasura. With each of her sighs she created battalions of female warriors, who destroyed the demonic army.

Furious at having lost the first round of battle, Mahisasura transformed himself into a buffalo to conquer the goddess. But Durga slew the buffalo and every other ferocious manifestation the chief of the demons assumed in order to fight her. At last, Durga drank from a wine cup given to her by the gods, and, surging with spiritual strength from the draught, cut off Mahisasura's head.

The gods praised Durga for having killed the chief of the demons, but her victory was not the end of the war. Two other powerful demons—Sumbha and Nisumbha— arose to challenge the gods, and once more the goddess was petitioned to go into battle.

Durga transformed herself into Parvati, Shiva's lovely consort, and decided that yet another goddess should confront Sumbha and Nisumbha. Durga-Parvati thus created Kalika, who sat herself atop Mount Himalaya and waited for the demons to come to her.

Sumbha and Nisumbha's chief servants disguised themselves in a disarmingly pleasing form, climbed the Himalayas, and there found the most beautiful goddess. They soon returned to their masters and told Sumbha: "O King, a most beautiful woman dwells there, shedding a radiance on Mount Himalaya. Never has such beauty been seen. Find out who the goddess is, O Lord, and take possession of her. A jewel, of exquisite limbs, illumining the four quarters with her luster, O Lord of Demons. All the precious gems, the elephant, horses and treasures of the Three Worlds have been brought together in your house. . . . Why is this beautiful jewel of a woman not seized by you?"[1]

Sumbha then sent a great demon as his messenger to seduce Kalika, instructing him on all the ways he should flatter the goddess to convince her to come to him. The demon went on his mission and, at his seductive best, tried to lure Kalika to descend the mountain to meet with Sumbha and Nisumbha, citing their powers and lordship over the world. However, Kalika replied serenely:

"What you say is true. Sumbha and Nisumbha are indeed powerful lords of the world. But how can I betray my own promise? Listen to the promise I have made to myself in my foolishness. He who conquers me in battle and removes my pride, he who is the match for my strength, he shall be my husband. So go and tell Sumbha or Nisumbha to come and conquer me here, and if they do so they can claim my hand."

The emissary demon tried to convince Kalika not to let her pride become a source of shame by causing her to be wrested from the mountaintop by the demons, but to go in dignity to them. Kalika would have none of it and insisted on remaining where she was.

Filled with indignation, the messenger returned and told Sumbha what Kalika had said. Sumbha, enraged, ordered his army chieftain to bring the goddess to him by force, dragging her down from the mountain by her hair.

The demon chieftain, accompanied by his army, found Kalika sitting on the mountain and ordered her to go with him to Sumbha and Nisumbha, threatening to drag her by the hair unless she consented.

Kalika answered, "If you will take me by force, what can I do?" The chieftain rushed toward her, but the goddess produced the sound *aum* with such strong vibrations that he was instantly reduced to ashes, whereupon her tiger destroyed the army.

When Sumbha learned that his chieftain and his army had been vanquished by the goddess, he sent two more of his servants, with an even larger army, to seize Kalika.

The demon army found the goddess sitting on her tiger, smiling gently. Some of the demons rushed forward to capture her, while others stood poised to attack her with bows and arrows. At this Kalika swelled with immense rage, and her face darkened until it became as black as ink. From her frowning forehead sprang forth the awesome goddess Kali, armed with a sword and a noose. Holding a skull-topped staff, with a garland of skulls at her throat and a tiger skin wrapped around her waist, Kali lolled her red tongue out of her wide mouth, frightening even the demons. Laughing terribly, she devoured the demon army. Eating elephants along with their riders, swallowing chariots and horses, crushing demons and animals under her feet, she struck with her sword and slew with her staff until the entire army was destroyed.

One great demon unleashed a hail of arrows, another hurled discuses by the hundreds, but Kali swallowed them all and laughed with rage. Mounted on her tiger, she rushed at the first demon, grabbed him by the hair, and decapitated him, then killed the second as he rushed at her. She then brought the heads of the two demons to Durga.

Next, Sumbha himself set out to kill Kali with the largest army yet. Kali emitted the sound *aum,* which filled the four corners of the earth, her tiger roared mightily, and the goddess plucked her bowstring and rang her bell to summon all the gods to battle. The gods multiplied themselves and the demons were slashed through, dispersed with holy water, and frightened off by the powerful laughter of Shiva, chief of the gods.

The mighty demonic warrior Raktabija remained, and Kali, after killing him, drank again and again of the *raktabija,* or seed blood, that gave her strength. Following this dreadful battle with Sumbha's army, Kali killed Nisumbha.

Now there remained only Sumbha himself. The demon and the goddess fought first with their weapons and then in close hand-to-hand combat. Sumbha seized her and sprang up into the sky, dragging her behind him. The two fought

so fiercely that they astonished all the divinities, gods and demons alike, and their battle would be remembered forever. At last Sumbha fell from the sky, pierced by her dart.

The gods, now triumphant, gathered around Kali to praise her for the war fought against the demons:

> *Salutations, O Narayani.*
> *Thine is the power of creation, preservation and dissolution.*
> *Thou art eternal. Thou art the Ground of Being.*
> *Thou art the Energies of Nature.*
> *Salutations, O Narayani.*
> *Thou who workest the salvation of those in suffering and*
> *distress who take refuge in Thee.*
> *Thou, O Devi, who removes the suffering of all….*
>
> *Who is there but Thyself in the sciences,*
> *in the Scriptures, and in the Vedic sayings*
> *that light the lamp of understanding.*
>
> *O Queen of the universe, protector of the universe,*
> *support of the universe.*
> *Thou art the goddess worthy to be adored*
> *by the Lord of the universe.*
> *Those who bow to Thee in devotion*
> *become the refuge of the universe.*

O Devi, be Thou pleased, and grant us protection
from the fear of foes forever,
as Thou hast protected us now by the destruction of the asuras.
Destroy all the sins of all the worlds and the great calamities
that have arisen through the maturing of evil portents.[2]

The world was at peace again: The skies cleared, the rivers flowed once more, and there was sweet singing, dancing, and rejoicing as the gods regained control of the world. The sacred fires burned anew; the sun shone on the world as it recovered its equilibrium. The goddess Durga departed, promising the gods that in times of need she would nourish the world from the vegetation grown on her body, and that Kali, her frightening other self, would always bless her worshipers and save them from their enemies.

Myth and Meaning in Today's World

Kali's myth represents the triumph of the feminine force over masculine power gone awry: When power is usurped by darker energies—symbolized in the myth by the demons—only the feminine can restore balance and harmony. The story can also be read as a cautionary tale about the dominance of patriarchy, which annihilates the feminine and can only be overthrown by the destructive-creative powers of the feminine. Esther Harding, the famous Jungian analyst and author, says of Kali: "Her divine power does not depend on her relation to a husband-god, and thus her actions are not dependent on the need to conciliate such a one or to accord with his qualities and attitudes. For she bears her identity in her own right."[3]

Even though Kali was born from Durga's brow, she is still one with Durga, as the Goddess in Hindu mythology can take on many manifestations, each with a different name and characteristic. The Durga-Kali manifestation is the most richly symbolic of female power, because it represents the archetype of creator-destroyer. Rather than a duality of two opposing forces, the creator-destroyer is perhaps the most truly feminine of all archetypes, as it represents the unique power all women have both to create (through birth and manifestation) and to destroy (through the menstrual cycle) in order to create anew. Kali's myth is in essence a tale of destruction and creation: There can be no harmony unless the forces of darkness that are ruling the world oppressively are first destroyed; only then can a new creation arise out of the ashes of the old.

Kali

We can see this principle at play in world events today, with the need for oppressive regimes to be destroyed before freedom and a new, more harmonious order can be established. Battles and wars are to be waged—mighty strength must be employed—and then a period of peacekeeping and reconstruction can give way to a more equitable system. War, in this sense, is a means to better the lives of innocent people suffering at the hands of dictators or under hostile regimes. The seeds of hope for a just society, better values, and greater dignity for the people are planted amid the efforts and losses of war. This is, in concrete terms, the archetype of the creator-destroyer at work in world affairs today, the Hindu myth of Kali in contemporary reality.

In many rituals Kali is described as being naked or sky-clad, and the absence of clothes denotes the absence of illusion; in her nakedness Kali does not hide the truth. She is also sometimes depicted in statues or paintings as full-breasted like a primordial Mother Goddess: This emphasizes her aspect as the creator, the mother who rescues her children when they are in danger and need. Her garland of fifty severed heads—each one a letter of the Sanskrit alphabet—is her repository of knowledge and wisdom.

Each Sanskrit letter is also believed to be the symbol of a sacred sound or vibration that keeps the world in harmony, another of Kali's functions. Her three eyes represent past, present, and future.

In India, the black goddess of death, who decapitates her enemies and adorns herself with their body parts, is worshiped as a great positive force, the embodiment of motherly compassion and kindness. Kali is the benevolent destroyer who will come to rescue her children from misfortune and evil, who will annihilate the dark forces and restore harmony. There are many rituals, songs, devotional acts, forms of worship, meditations, and sacred sounds that Hinduism has developed over the centuries to honor and worship Kali. She is a powerful presence not only in Hindu myth but in ordinary households, where her powers of destruction and creation are called upon to restore balance to everyday affairs.

Kali Tantras

One of the central themes of the eternal religion of Hinduism—the core of sacred understanding—is Tantra, a series of holy texts featuring the discourses of Shiva and Shakti. Along with the Vedas, the Puranas, and the *Bhagavad-Gita*—the other fundamental holy texts and teachings of Hinduism—Tantra describes the divine energy and creative power that makes up the universe.

Tantra arose in India in about the tenth century CE, and both Hinduism and Tibetan Buddhism adopted some of its principles, although it was originally a separate religious current. It was an esoteric system of scriptures and ideas, and adepts had to undergo an initiation in order to study Tantra. The main principle is that worldly things, usually considered an obstacle to spiritual awakening, need not become barriers if they are properly understood and transformed. Tantric texts offer complex rituals, prayers, meditations, and disciplines for the attainment of spiritual power, which transforms worldly experience from secular to sacred.

In tantric texts, Shiva and Shakti, in her form as his consort Parvati, sit on two clouds high above in the heavens, and Parvati poses a series of questions regarding the fundamental principles of the universe; Shiva answers his wife not only by describing the principles but by manifesting them. Each of the tantric texts is organized around five themes: (1) the creation of the world; (2) its destruction or dissolution; (3) the worship of the godhead in its masculine or feminine aspect; (4) the attainment of supernatural abilities; and (5) the various methods of achieving union with the supreme by meditation. Tantras, or sacred practices, are invariably accompanied by yantras, sacred symbols, and mantras, sacred sounds; thus the meditations take a complex form: Each must follow certain principles and include elaborate visualizations and chants of sacred sounds.

It is in the *Yogini Tantra*, one the most famous of the holy tantric texts, that Shiva first tells of Kali. The goddess of creation and dissolution seems the perfect divinity for Tantra, the system that dissolves obstacles preventing spiritual growth and creates new conditions for the nurturing of enlightenment. The twenty-eight chapters of the *Yogini Tantra* open with Shiva's eulogy of Kali as the cosmic mother, in which he describes her as dark as a thunderstorm, wearing a garland and waistband of skulls, with disheveled hair and completely naked. The *Yogini Tantra* is divided into nine *patalas*, or foundation principles, that explain the sacred practices and rituals associated with worshiping the goddess. Note that this Tantra contains in its title the word "yogini," meaning female practitioner. It is a sacred text that teaches women all the sacred and secret ways of calling Kali powers to themselves and petitioning the goddess to manifest in their lives.

First Patala

Parvati tells Shiva that she has listened to the exposition of Tantras (sacred practices) before, but would like to learn more from her consort, who is also her teacher. In answer, Shiva says that he will teach the *Yogini Tantra*, the giver of wealth and liberation. This knowledge is to be kept secret from all minor deities, demons, and supernatural beings.

The *Yogini Tantra* is the worship of the Great Goddess, who must be imagined as described in the eulogy—dark, disheveled, naked, and garlanded with skulls. In this vision she has an open mouth with lolling tongue, makes a terrifying roar, and stares from three red eyes. She wears the crescent moon on her forehead, earrings made of two

corpses, and adornments of gems as bright as the full moon. Laughing loudly, she spurts two streams of blood. In three of her four arms she holds a cleaver, a decapitated head, and an arrow, and her fourth hand is poised in a sacred gesture that dispels fears and grants wishes. She is sometimes seen sitting on the corpse of Shiva having intercourse with him. After describing the image to be held in mind, Shiva tells Parvati that devotion to the goddess must be like devotion to a guru or to one's family in order for the sacred practices to be effective.

Second Patala

Parvati requests that Shiva speak of Kali. He declares that Kali is the greatest of the great teachers, supreme in knowledge and the bringer of liberation. Her disciples include even the supreme gods of Hindu mythology, Brahma, Vishnu, and himself. If an initiate, or yogini, recites a mantra to Kali with firm conviction, she will become Kali. Once the power of the goddess has been called with the mantra, a ritual is performed in her honor. The beads used for the ritual should be made of bone from human skulls for long-lasting success, or cut from crystal or rubies. The full circlet should have 108 beads, and the *meru*, the bead that marks the beginning and end of the rosary, should be made of a king's tooth. The mantra should be repeated 108 times, and each bead should be held in turn while the mantra is being recited. The best place to worship Kali is the cremation ground, and the ritual is to be performed at the full moon and new moon.

Third Patala

Next, Parvati asks how the yogini can protect herself from calamities and illnesses. Shiva explains that a protective talisman can be made from bark cut on the eighth night of the waxing moon and held overnight inside a golden container. Even a small piece of bark can protect against negative energies.

Shiva explains that while this is done, the yogini should envision Kali unclothed. Garb represents a form of masking or deceit, thus the image of the nude Kali helps dispel illusion, which can be the source of negative thoughts that lead to sickness and misfortune.

Fourth Patala

Parvati then asks which issues of life Kali is best able to affect. Shiva replies that Kali can help the yogini attain

greater knowledge, wealth, and influence, and he outlines
the goddess's six ways of giving aid: pacifying, subduing,
causing enmity, driving away, uprooting, and ultimately,
causing death. The yogini should identify which method
best suits the situation and then petition the goddess.

Fifth Patala

Shiva explains in this Patala where the Kali practices,
or Tantras, should be performed in order to attain their
perfect mastery. Certain places are more appropriate than
others for Kali Tantras, as the energy of the goddess is more
readily accessible at these sites. Her favorite locations are
cremation grounds, deserts, riverbanks, mountains, cross-
roads, at the root of a tree, or in any locale where there is a
lingam (Shiva's phallic stone, found in many Hindu temples).
Kali's devotions should be performed in lonely spots,
undisturbed by the presence of anyone but the devotee.

Sixth Patala

Parvati wishes to learn about the different bodily power
spots yoginis should concentrate on when practicing Kali
Tantras. Shiva explains that they are divided into three

categories: divine, for cultivating spiritual qualities of meditation and enlightenment; heroic, for confronting situations that need courage, such as sacrificing something important to obtain harmony or health; and ordinary, for maintaining a balanced, harmonious life. The meditations are secret and may not be told to anyone. They should focus on three different power spots that are to be imagined on the body of Kali as a sixteen-year-old girl. The first spot extends from the feet to the vagina, the second from the hips to the breasts, and the third from the breasts to the head. By concentrating the meditation on these three areas of the body in turn, the yogini can unleash a great coil of energy—the kundalini—which rises through the spinal cord to the top of the head. Shiva calls this the great nectar—the bounty of the supreme *shakti* within the body.

Seventh Patala

The next teaching elucidates the great powers the Kali Tantras can give a yogini: She will be able to move and act in her sleep, manifest her dreams and wishes as living realities, attract whatever she desires, cross great distances without effort, achieve a lucid dream state, and even attain the power to heal the sick and restore the dead to life.

Eighth Patala

When a yogini projects herself into an adversary's imagination, Shiva tells Parvati, she appears terrifying, with blazing eyes and fifty faces, thus frightening enemies away simply by appearing in their minds.

Ninth Patala

Shiva concludes the teachings of the Kali Tantra by saying that the Great Goddess is the ultimate Mother of Everything. As such she has an immense form that contains all knowledge, all bliss, all spiritual paths, all desires: in short, everything. The ultimate meditation is that in which the self is melted into the essence of everything.

The Kali Tantras are powers that have been studied and cultivated in India for many hundreds of years and constitute a body of spiritual training for devotees of the goddess. They are rarely written about and described in Western texts, yet are essential to the knowledge of Kali.

Kali Yantras and Mantras

Yantras are sacred, mandala-shaped symbols used in Tantric meditations to evoke a particular aspect of the goddess. Mantras are sacred sounds that when intoned can also evoke certain of her characteristics. This section outlines Kali yantras, mantras, and accompanying meditations that are to be used together as a visualized prayer to call a certain incarnation of Kali to you. The meditations focus on images of Kali that must be visualized while reciting the mantra. These very ancient practices are still followed today by Kali devotees. The yantras are drawn in chalk at the entrance of Kali temples as well as in household or cave shrines dedicated to the goddess throughout India.

These yantras can also be drawn on your own home altar or on a piece of paper; you might want to place the statuette of Kali that you find in this box on one of these symbols. It will draw power to the goddess and keep her always "charged." You may also use the yantras alone as shields or talismans—drawings that you can fold and take with you in your purse or pocket or place under your pillow at night. They will protect you with the fierceness of Kali herself.

Kali

Drawing a yantra on a piece of paper before beginning the meditation focuses the ritual. It is also a symbolic reminder of the power of the meditation that can be drawn upon for hours and days afterward. All yantras, mantras, and meditations included herewith are equally powerful, but one may work better than the others at certain times. Instinct is the best guide in choosing the Kali meditation that will work for you at a specific time.

Kali

MEDITATION: Two-armed, dark-hued, very terrifying, horrible, screaming, formidable, with a garland of skulls, swelling breasts, a cleaver in her right hand while the left makes a threatening gesture. The backdrop is a cremation ground.

MANTRA: *Om Hrim Kali Kali Mahakali Kaun Mahyam Dehi Svaha.*

Kapalini

MEDITATION: Black, beautiful face, disheveled hair, seated on four heads, showing a cleaver and a trident, bestowing good luck and dispelling fear.

MANTRA: *Om Hrim Krim Kapalini Maha-kapala-priye-manase kapala-siddim me Phat Svaha.*

Kulla

MEDITATION: Four-armed, with three eyes, seated with severed heads on a corpse, bestowing good luck and dispelling fear with her two left hands. In her right hands she holds a book and prayer beads.

MANTRA: *Om Krim Kullaya Namah.*

Kurukulla

MEDITATION: Large, rising breasts, beautiful black face, seated on a corpse, disheveled hair, wearing a garland of skulls, carrying a cleaver and a shield.

MANTRA: *Krim Om Kurukulle Hrim Ma Sarva-Jana-Vasamanya Krim Kurukulle Hrim.*

Virodhini

MEDITATION: Full, rising breasts, wearing a garland of snakes and bones, terrifying, with three eyes and arms, holding a trident, a noose made with a snake, and a dagger. Clothed in yellow, seated on a corpse.

MANTRA: *Om Krim Hrim Klim Hum Virodhi satrun-ucchataya virodhaya satru-Hum Phat.*

Vipracitta

MEDITATION: Four arms, naked, body the color of a blue lotus, full breasts, disheveled hair, lolling tongue, inspiring fear; holds a cleaver, a severed head, a skullcap, and a trident. She shows her teeth and blood flows from the corner of her mouth.

Kali

MANTRA: *Om Shrim Klim Camunde Vipracitta Dushta-Gatini Shatrun-Nashaya Etad-Dina Siddhim Me Dehi Hum Phat Svaha.*

Ugra

MEDITATION: Naked, formidable, with terrible face, wearing a garland of skulls, black, four arms, holding an image of a swastika (an ancient Hindu symbol of infinite power long before it was adopted by the Nazi movement), a night lotus, a skull, and a knife. Kali in this form dwells in the ground.

MANTRA: *Om Strim Hum Hrim Phat.*

Ugraprabha

MEDITATION: Skin the color of a white lotus, seated on a corpse, naked, with disheveled hair, pleasant face, four arms, three eyes, eating carcasses, wearing a girdle of severed hands, holding a cleaver, a decapitated head, a skull bowl, and a knife.

MANTRA: *Om Hum Ugra-Prabhe Devi Kali Ma Svarupam Darshaya Hum Phat Svaha.*

Dipa Nitya

MEDITATION: Three eyes like large sapphires, with a garland of skulls, disheveled hair, fearsome fangs, armlets of human bone, bracelets of skulls, four arms, carrying a cleaver and a decapitated head in her two left hands and showing the gestures of giving and of dispelling fear with her right hands.

MANTRA: *Om Krim Hum Diptayai Sarva-Mantra-Phaladayai Hum Phat Svaha.*

Making Your Own Kali Ritual

Kali is a very powerful goddess of creation and destruction who can help you end or destroy negative patterns that keep you from experiencing well-being and freedom. Whenever you find yourself facing a difficult situation that you must bring to an end in order for a pattern to change and return to harmony, you can call on Kali's powers.

Place the statuette on the altar provided in this box or in any power spot in your home, preferably somewhere dark and secret, away from the influence of all other objects and people. You may want to choose one of the locations outlined in the Fifth Patala of the *Yogini Tantra*, perhaps a cave or the root of a tree, or if you have a pond or fountain in your garden you may set up your altar and meditation place close to its waters (see page 59).

Kali rituals should be performed at night only, on the full moon or the new moon. Consult a moon calendar to choose the night of your ritual, and gather your energy while you wait for that particular night by focusing on what needs to end and what needs to be born in the situation you are contemplating. Review the Fourth Patala of the *Yogini Tantra* (see page 57) and choose a method that seems appropriate to you for ending the situation. You will not, of course, choose "causing death" in any literal sense. That method of Kali's aid is only a metaphor for ending a negative cycle.

On the night of the ritual, find a time when you can be alone and quiet. Perhaps play some soft Indian music and burn incense sticks to put you in the mood. Choose one of the yantras on pages 64 through 69 and draw it on a piece of paper, then place it under the Kali figurine. Now visualize the form of the goddess that goes with that particular yantra: Imagine the terrifying presence of the goddess in her fullness, feel her energy rising within you as you gently chant the accompanying mantra. You must not rush this meditation, but rather allow a full half-hour to an hour to complete it. It takes time to perfect the visualization, and you can only ask for Kali's help once she has fully revealed herself to you in your mind's eye. The yantra is a graphic, magical form of the meditation you are visualizing. You can keep the piece of paper with the yantra drawn on it to remind you of the power and feeling of that particular visualization.

Once you hold Kali in your inner vision, softly speak to her and explain the situation that needs to be solved by her destructive-creative powers. Ask her to annihilate your problem with the force of her fullness and to end it, giving rise to a new, more potent harmony. Put your full intention behind your words and breathe deeply as you do so. Now, holding the energy of your intent, breathing slowly as you concentrate, gradually focus on the three Kali spots outlined in the Sixth Patala on page 59: First concentrate your energy on the area that extends from the feet to the vagina. Do this slowly, until you feel this part of your body vibrate with the vision. Then concentrate on the area from the hips to the breasts, and thirdly from the breasts to the head. Ideally, you should feel your whole body vibrate or tingle as it is awakened. This is a sure sign that the kundalini energy is uncoiling and moving through your body. If you are sitting, rock your body gently back and forth during this part of the meditation. If you are standing, gently shake your body and allow it to move with the energy. This is your very own ritual, and no one will see

you; it is your time to be with yourself, so let go and relax into the meditation and the sounds of the music.

After you have asked Kali for help, honor her with a few words and slowly conclude the ritual. You may want to recite one of the poems in the following section to end the meditation. Keep the yantra drawing folded under your pillow that night and on subsequent ones until you are certain the problem is being solved by the powers you have invoked during your ritual.

Kali rituals are excellent for putting an end to issues, relationships, or partnerships that have fallen into a negative trend and bring unhappiness. We need to realize that we inevitably play a part in every negative situation in which we find ourselves. First we must analyze the ways in which we nourish and give energy to the unhappy issue, and subsequently we must think of alternative, happier ways that can feed the relationship in positive ways. Often, there needs to be a "death," an ending to the habits and actions that feed unhappiness before a new relationship can be established. In asking for help to end the negativity, you ask Kali to help you put a stop to what you are doing to perpetuate it. This determination demands courage and clarity of focus, because we fear that we may lose something by ending a situation. Kali helps us to see that what is lost is only the negative and what is gained is the positive.

Kali Songs and Poetry

Kali is so well loved in India that a whole literary genre of songs and devotional poetry has developed in her honor. In Calcutta stands the main Kali temple in India, a cremation ground for Hindu families on the shores of the sacred river Ganges. Families and friends gather here to cremate the deceased on wooden pyres and then throw the ashes into the Ganges with Kali's blessings. One of the Kali myths recounts that a god became enraged at her powers and cut her into many pieces that fell in different parts of the Indian subcontinent. Her vagina is supposed to have fallen in Calcutta, thus her main temple was built there. The greatest tradition of Kali poetry and song was developed here and in the surrounding region of Bengal around the mid-eighteenth century. It is rich with poems of battle, hymns to Kali as the goddess of transformation, and poems in defiance of death.

Terrible-faced, horrible, with disheveled hair and four arms,
Divine, adorned with a necklace of sliced heads;
Holding in Her two left hands a freshly hacked head and a cleaver,

Kali

And in Her right hand displaying the "fear not"
and boon-bestowing hand gestures;
Lustrously black like a large cloud, and robed with nothing but the sky,
Anointed with blood dripping down from the necklace of heads at Her
Throat;
Terrible because of the pair of children's corpses She wears for earrings,
Her teeth horrid and Her face frightful, but her breasts high and uplifted;
A skirt of cut arms hanging from Her waist, laughter bellowing out,
Her face shining from the red stream dripping from the two corners of Her
Mouth;
Shouting terribly, dwelling on the very fierce cremation grounds,
Her third eye permeated with the newly risen sun;
With fangs for teeth and a pearl necklace that swings to the right as She
Moves,
Sitting on the Great Lord [Shiva], who has taken the form of a corpse;
Surrounded by jackals and their terrible, all-pervading cries,
Engaging Great Time in the act of reversed sexual intercourse;
Her face happy and pleased, like a lotus—
He who thinks on Kali thus will have all his wishes fulfilled[4]

What a joke!
She's a young woman
from a good family
yes, but
She's naked—and flirts, hips cocked
When She stands.

With messy hair
roars awful and grim
this gentlewoman tramples demons
in a corpse-strewn battle.
But the God of Love
looks and swoons.

While ghosts, ghouls, and goblins
from Shiva's retinue, and Her own companions
nude just like Her
dance and frolic on the field,
She swallows elephants
chariots and charioteers
striking terror into the hearts
of gods, demons, and men.

She walks fast,
enjoying Herself tremendously.
Human arms hang from her waist.

Ramprasad says: Mother Kali,
preserver of the world,
have mercy!
Take the burden
ferry me across this ocean of becoming.
Oh woman,
destroy my sorrows.
—Ramprasad Sen [5]

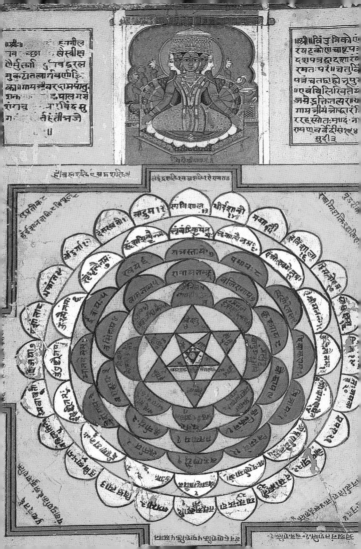

Is my Mother Kali really black?
People say Kali is black,
but my heart doesn't agree.
If She's black,
How can she light up the world?
Sometimes my Mother is white,
Sometimes yellow, blue, and red.
I cannot fathom Her.
My whole life has passed
Trying.

She is Matter,
then Spirit,
then complete Void.

It's easy to see
How Kamalakanta [the poet]
Went crazy.
—Kamalakanta Bhattacarya [6]

Wherever there's a woman in any Bengali home
doing her work
screening her smiles with her veil,
she is You, Ma [Mother];
she is You, Black Goddess.

Kali

Carefully rising with the light of dawn
to attend with softened hands
to household chores,
she is You, Ma;
she is You, Black Goddess.

The woman who gives alms, makes vows, does worship, reads scriptures
all correctly and with a smile
who drapes her sari over the child on her lap
soothing its hunger with a lullaby,
she is You, Ma;
she is You, Black Goddess.

She can't be anyone else;
mother, father, sister, housewife
all are You.
Even at death
smiling
You make the journey with us.
My mind knows this, and my heart as well:
she is You, Ma;
she is You, Black Goddess.
—Ma Basanti Cakrabartti[7]

Notes to the Text

1 Mookerjee, Ajit. *Kali: The Feminine Force*. Rochester, VT: Destiny Books, 1988, p. 52.

2 Ibid. pp. 56–57.

3 Harding, Esther M. *Women's Mysteries, Ancient and Modern*. Boston: Shambhala Publications, 1976, p. 125.

4 McDermott, Rachel Fell. *Singing to the Goddess: Poems to Kali and Uma from Bengal*. New York: Oxford University Press, 2001, p. 19.

5 Ibid. pp. 22–23.

6 Ibid. p. 39.

7 Ibid. pp. 45–46.

Further Reading

Harding, Esther M. *Women's Mysteries, Ancient and Modern*. Boston: Shambhala Publications, 1976

Hixon, Lex. *Mother of the Universe: Visions of the Goddess and Tantric Hymns of Enlightenment*. Wheaton, IL: Quest Books, 1994

McDermott, Rachel Fell. *Singing to the Goddess: Poems to Kali and Uma from Bengal*. New York: Oxford University Press, 2001

Mookerjee, Ajit. *Kali: The Feminine Force*. Rochester, VT: Destiny Books, 1988

Swami Satyananda Saraswati. *Kali Puja*. Napa, CA: Devi Mandir, 1988

The Encyclopedia of Eastern Philosophy and Religion. Boston: Shambhala Publications, 1994

Woodroffe, John. *Hymns to the Goddess/Hymns to Kali*. Twin Lakes, WI: Lotus Press, 1981

Art Acknowledgments

BOX, CASE WRAP: *The Goddess Durga as Badhrakali.* India, Himachal Pradesh, Basohli, ca. 1675. Los Angeles County Museum of Art.

COPYRIGHT, TABLE OF CONTENTS: *Durga Slaying the Buffalo Demon.* India, Himachal Pradesh, Guler, ca. 1750–1775. Los Angeles County Museum of Art.

PLATFORM: Pepita Seth, London. Alvin O. Bellak collection, Philadelphia Museum of Art.

ENDPAPERS: Alvin O. Bellak collection, Philadelphia Museum of Art.

TITLE PAGE, PAGE 12: *Durga.* India, Himachal Pradesh, Basohli, late 17th century, Los Angeles County Museum of Art.

PAGE 4: *The Great Goddess Durga Slaying the Buffalo Demon.* Philadelphia Museum of Art.

PAGE 8-9: Private collection.

PAGE 14: Private collection.

PAGE 16: St. Petersburg Branch of the Institute of Oriental Studies, Russia.

PAGE 19: Barry Miller collection.

PAGE 22: Private collection.

PAGE 26: Alvin O. Bellak collection, Philadelphia Museum of Art.

PAGE 29: Robin Hamilton, London.

PAGE 32: *The Goddess Kali* by Richard B. Godfrey. ca. 1770. Los Angeles County Museum of Art.

PAGE 35: C.L. Bhrany collection, New Delhi.

PAGE 36: C.L. Bhrany collection, New Delhi.

PAGE 39: C.L. Bhrany collection, New Delhi.

PAGE 40: C.L. Bhrany collection, New Delhi.

PAGE 42–43: Alvin O. Bellak collection, Philadelphia Museum of Art.

PAGE 47: C.L. Bhrany collection, New Delhi.

PAGE 50: Alvin O. Bellak collection, Philadelphia Museum of Art.

PAGE 52: *Durga Being Worshipped by Two Devotees.* India, Rajastan, Kota, ca. 1850. Los Angeles County Museum of Art.

PAGE 54–55: C.L. Bhrany collection, New Delhi.

PAGE 58: *Durga Attacking the Elephant, Buffalo, Lion, and Human Forms of Mahisha, Folio from a Markandeya Purana.* India, Himachal Pradesh, Guler, ca. 1760. Los Angeles County Museum of Art.

PAGE 62: C.L. Bhrany collection, New Delhi.

PAGE 66: Daniel Benveniste collection, San Francisco.

PAGE 70–71: *Religious Procession: Kali.* India, West Bengal, Murshidabad, ca. 1850. Los Angeles County Museum of Art.